THE BIRTHDAY·ABC

THE BIRTHDAY ABC

ERIC METAXAS · TIM RAGLIN

SIMON & SCHUSTER BOOKS FOR YOUNG READERS

SIMON & SCHUSTER BOOKS FOR YOUNG READERS

An imprint of Simon & Schuster Children's Publishing Division

1230 Avenue of the Americas, New York, New York 10020

SIMON & SCHUSTER BOOKS FOR YOUNG READERS is a trademark of Simon & Schuster.

Book design by Anahid Hamparian

The text for this book is set in Caslon 224. The illustrations were done in pen and ink.

Manufactured in the United States of America

10 9 8 7 6 5 4 3 2 1

Library of Congress Cataloging-in-Publication Data

Metaxas, Eric.

The birthday ABC / by Eric Metaxas ; illustrated by Tim Raglin.   p.   cm.

Summary: Animals from A to Z help the reader celebrate a birthday.

1. Birthdays—Juvenile poetry.   2. Children's poetry, American.   3. Alphabet rhymes.

[1. Birthdays—Poetry.   2. Animals—Poetry.   3. American poetry.   4. Alphabet.]

I. Raglin, Tim, ill.   II. Title.

PS3563.E8137B57   1995   811'.54—dc20   [E]   93-46896   CIP   AC

ISBN: 0-671-88306-2

For Mark and Mike, with love

—T.R. and E.M.

A is for the Alligator,
who accidentally ate his waiter.
"Oh, dear!" he said. "It's my mistake!
But may I have some birthday cake?"

B is for the circus Bear,
who hasn't anything to wear.
It's plain to see he's quite astute
to greet you in his birthday suit.

C is for the jet-black Crow,
who fancies silver, as you know.
He's brought you some this special day
to help you eat your curds and whey.

D is for the Dromedary
and the hump that he must carry.
It's just the thing to sit astride
when going on your birthday ride.

E is for the noble Elephant,
whose nose is long and rather elegant.
It's also just a trifle loud
in summoning the birthday crowd!

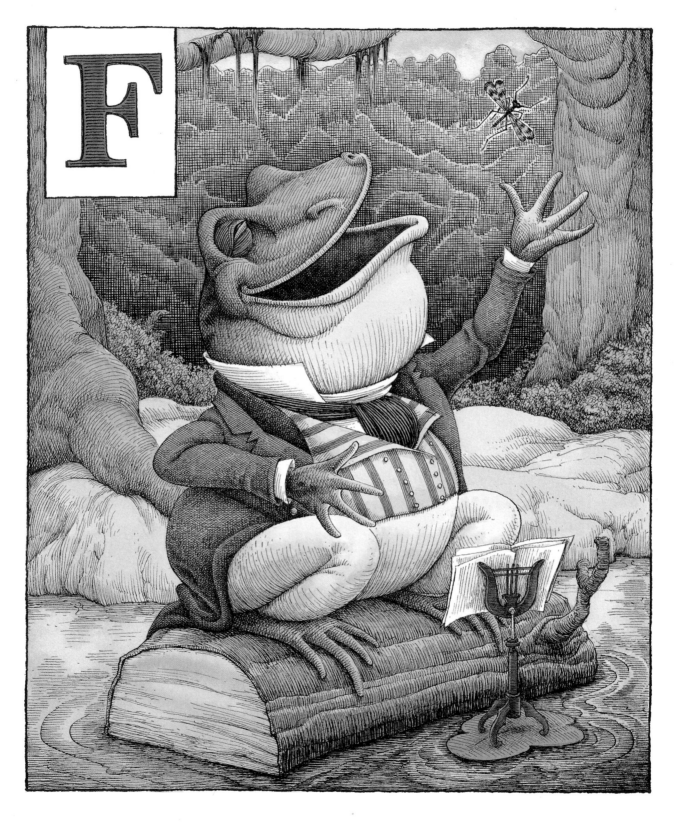

F is for the croaking Frog,
muttering upon his log.
This day, however, loud and clear,
he croons a song of birthday cheer!

G is for the tall Giraffe,
who has a long and throaty laugh.
It's quite contagious, as you'll hear,
in celebrating your new year.

H is for the leaping Hare,
who's often neither here nor there.
He's here today, tho', as you see,
to join your birthday company.

I is for the great Iguana,
greenest member of the fauna,
announcing to the congregation
your Happy Birthday proclamation!

J is for the jesting Jackal
with his loud, familiar cackle.
But now he's quiet and sincere
in saying, "Happy birthday, dear."

K is for the Kangaroo,
who's wrapped her gift in red and blue.
The bow is white and nicely tied,
but tell me, madame, *what's inside?*

L is for the kingly Lion
and his son, the princely scion.
These rulers of the jungle wild
today salute the birthday child!

M is for the stately Moose,
whose birthday drink is apple juice.
He hoists aloft his golden cup,
and now he toasts you—*bottoms up!*

N is for the crested Newt,
who woos you in his Sunday suit.
He hopes you'll think him quite the dandy
for bringing you this birthday candy.

O is for Orangutan,
who from a limb is seen to hang.
He's bringing biscuits in a tin,
and shortly will be dropping in.

P is for the Porcupine,
whose quills are sharp and very fine.
With ink and paper now he'll write
a birthday poem in verses bright.

Q is for the humble Quail,
whose voice is raised to no avail.
Through other means he shall be heard—
a birthday speech without a word.

R is for the snorting Rhino,
whose longer name both you and I know.
He tries to sound his silent horn
to mark the day when you were born!

S is for the barking Seal,
who's waiting for his noonday meal.
He loathes the thought of being tardy
for your gala birthday party.

T is for the trudging Tortoise,
trying gently to exhort us.
"Clear your throats and come along!
It's time to sing the birthday song!"

U is for the Unicorn,
    a beast in myth and folklore born.
He isn't found in any zoo,
    but comes this day to visit you.

V is for the grizzled Vulture,
a vulgar chap with little culture.
But on his birthday, as I've heard,
he's quite a smart and dapper bird.

W is for the Weasel,
cunning master of the easel.
Ask politely and he'll do
a birthday portrait just for you.

X is here to mark the spot
where animals are always not.
But absence is a thing quite pleasant
when it holds your birthday present.

Y is for the shaggy Yak,
 bowed beneath his heavy pack.
His smile, however, is hard to hide—
he knows your birthday gift's inside.

Z is for the final Zebra,
tail end of the alphabet!
If there's a rhyme to go with it,
I guess I haven't found it yet.
Have you?